A Mother's Yea

Editor

Mary McKinnon McSwain,

Francis McKinnon Morton

Alpha Editions

This edition published in 2023

ISBN : 9789357936767

Design and Setting By
Alpha Editions
www.alphaedis.com
Email - info@alphaedis.com

Contents

PREFACE

This little volume has been compiled for mothers and is lovingly offered as a tribute to the memory of the almost perfect mother whose love cradled my own childhood so sweetly as to make all motherhood forever more dear to me.

It seems to be true that the years of a woman's life that sink deepest into her heart and are fraught with her keenest joy and pain are the years when her little children are clinging about her skirts. Then it is that she is truly "wealthy with small cares, and small hands clinging to her knees." But then, too, she is often too busy with the passing of the full days and the long nights, so often punctuated by the restless clinging of rosy fingers and all the dear demands of babyhood, to realize fully how blest are the days through which she is living.

It is especially for the busy mother that I have gathered this little collection of beautiful thoughts about childhood and motherhood, from some of the world's best thinkers.

I hope it may bring to some of them as much pleasure in the reading as it has to me in the preparation.

The selections from the writings of Lucy Larcom, Holmes, Whittier, Longfellow, Emerson, Lowell, Celia Thaxter, and Edith Thomas are used by the courteous permission of the authorized publishers of these writers, the Houghton Mifflin Company.

The selections from the writings of Robert Louis Stevenson are from "A Child's Garden of Verses."

The selection from Sidney Lanier is taken from "The Poems of Sidney Lanier." Both are published by Charles Scribner's Sons and the selections are used by permission of that firm. The little poem from Eugene Field is also used by special arrangement with Charles Scribner's Sons, the authorized publishers of the works of Eugene Field.

The selections from the book called "The Finest Baby in the World" are used by the courtesy of its publishers, the Fleming H. Revell Company.

The selection from Ruth McEnery Stuart is taken from "Napoleon Jackson," published by the Century Company, and is used with their permission.

The selection from the writings of Lewis Carroll is taken from the "Adventures of Alice in Wonderland" and is used by permission of the publishers, the Macmillan Company.

Acknowledgment is also made to the Bobbs-Merrill Company for the use of the selections from the writings of James Whitcomb Riley, and to D. Appleton & Co. for the selections from Bryant.

Acknowledgment is due the courtesy of the New York *Sun* and the Denver *News* for the use of the selections credited to them.

An effort has been made to find the name and the author of each selection used so that proper credit could be given with each. This has not been always possible and I have chosen not to leave out a beautiful selection on that account.

George MacDonald says, "He who drops a beautiful thought into the heart of a friend gives as the angels do"; and Emerson says that "Next to the originator of a beautiful thought is the one who first quotes it." So I do not think that any one who has said anything beautiful about childhood would wish to be left out of a Mother's Year Book even if the credit for his work was not given quite correctly.

FRANCIS MCKINNON MORTON.

JANUARY

JANUARY FIRST

Where did you come from, Baby Dear?

Out of the Everywhere into the here.

. . . .

But how did you come to us, you Dear?

God thought of you and so I am here.

George MacDonald

JANUARY SECOND

What is the dream in the Baby's eyes

As he lies and blinks in a mute surprise?

. . . .

Bathed in the dawnlight, what does he see

That slow years have hidden from you and from me?

Tom Cordry

JANUARY THIRD

Little Life from out the life Divine,

Little heart so near and dear to mine,

Little bark, new-launched upon Life's sea

Floating o'er the tide to mine and me,

Little comer on our shore of time,

Little ray from out God's great sublime,

Little traveller from Eternity

May my love protect and shelter thee.

The Denver News

JANUARY FOURTH

What shall we wrap the Baby in?
Nothing that fingers have woven will do:
Looms of the heart weave ever anew:
Love, only Love is the right thread to spin
Love we must wrap the Baby in.
Lucy Larcom

JANUARY FIFTH

Look at me with thy large brown eyes,
Philip, my King!
For round thee the purple shadow lies
Of babyhood's regal dignities.
Lay on my neck thy tiny hand,
With Love's invisible scepter laden;
I am thine Esther to command,
Till thou shalt find thy queen-handmaiden,
Philip, my King!
Dinah Mulock Craik

JANUARY SIXTH

Nay, but our children in our midst,
What else but our hearts are they,
Walking on the ground?
If but the breeze blew harsh on one of them,
Mine eye says "No" to slumber all night long.
From the "Hamasah"
Hittan idnibn al-Mu'alla of Tayyi

JANUARY SEVENTH

We must take all our children bring us whether it
be Joy or Pain.
Auerbach

JANUARY EIGHTH

Oh child, what news from Heaven?
Swinburne

JANUARY NINTH

Sweet floweret, pledge o' meikle love,
And ward o' mony a prayer,
What heart o' stane wad thou na move,
Sae helpless, sweet and fair?
Robert Burns

JANUARY TENTH

His child's unsullied purity demands
The deepest reverence at a parent's hands.
Juvenal

JANUARY ELEVENTH

Little Gossip, blithe and hale,
Tattling many a broken tale,
Singing many a tuneless song,
Lavish of a heedless tongue,
Simple maid, void of art,

Babbling out thy very heart.

Ambrose Phillips

JANUARY TWELFTH

O child! O new-born denizen
Of Life's great city! On thy head
The glory, of the morn is shed
Like a celestial benison.

Longfellow

JANUARY THIRTEENTH

Ah! This taking to one's arms a little group of
souls, fresh from the hand of God, and living with
them in loving companionship through all their
stainless years is, or ought to be, like living in Heaven,
for of such is the Heavenly Kingdom.

J. G. Holland

JANUARY FOURTEENTH

The sun of dawn,
That brightens through the mother's tender eyes.

Tennyson

JANUARY FIFTEENTH

We are so dull and thankless; and too slow
To catch the sunshine till it slips away,
And now it seems surpassing strange to me
That while I wore the badge of Motherhood,

I did not kiss more oft and tenderly
The little child that brought me only good.
Mary Louise Riley Smith

JANUARY SIXTEENTH

Children are God's apostles, day by day
Sent forth to preach of Love and Hope and Peace.
Lowell

JANUARY SEVENTEENTH

She has forgotten her sufferings for joy that the
child is born.
Kipling

JANUARY EIGHTEENTH

A Baby's feet, like sea-shells pink,
Might tempt, should Heaven see meet,
An angel's lips to kiss, we think,
A Baby's feet.
Like rose-hued sea flowers, toward the heart
They stretch and spread and wink
Their ten soft buds that part and meet.
Swinburne

JANUARY NINETEENTH

Greek babies were like the babies of modern
Europe: equally troublesome, equally delightful to
their parents, equally uninteresting to the rest of

society.

Mahaffy

JANUARY TWENTIETH

They knew as I do now, what keen delight
A strong man feels to watch the tender flight
Of little children playing in his sight.

Edmund Gosse

JANUARY TWENTY-FIRST

The child would twine
A trustful hand, unasked in thine
And find his comfort in thy face.

Tennyson

JANUARY TWENTY-SECOND

This little seed of life and love,
Just lent us for a day.

Parsons

JANUARY TWENTY-THIRD

Pray for the infant's soul:
With its spirit crown unsoiled.

Philip James Bailey

JANUARY TWENTY-FOURTH

Child of brighter than the morning's birth,
And lovelier than all smiles that may be smiled

Save only of little children undefiled,
Sweet, perfect, witless of their own dear worth,
Like rose of love, mute melody of mirth,
Glad as a bird is when the woods are mild,
Adorable as is nothing save a child,
Hails with wide eyes and lips on earth,
His lovely life with all its heaven to be.
Swinburne

JANUARY TWENTY-FIFTH

Where has he gone to, Mother's boy,
Little plaid dresses and curls of joy?
Who is this Gentleman, haughty in glance
Walking around in a new pair of pants?
Folger McKinsey

JANUARY TWENTY-SIXTH

It is very nice to think
The world is full of meat and drink,
With little children saying grace
In every Christian kind of place.
Robert Louis Stevenson

JANUARY TWENTY-SEVENTH

Did truth on earth ever hide,
Hath innocence anywhere smiled,
Did purity anywhere bide,
They are found in the eyes of a child.

Harry Alexander Moore

JANUARY TWENTY-EIGHTH

Now he thinks he 'll go to sleep:
I can see the shadows creep
Over his eyes in soft eclipse,
Over his brow and over his lips,
Out to his little finger tips:
Softly sinking down he goes!
Down he goes! Down he goes!
See! He is hushed in sweet repose!

J. G. Holland

JANUARY TWENTY-NINTH

To what shall I liken her smiling
Upon me, her kneeling lover?
How it leaped from her lips to her eyelids,
And dimpled her wholly over,
Till her outstretched hands smiled also
And I almost seem to see
The very heart of her mother
Sending sun, through her veins, to me.

Lowell

JANUARY THIRTIETH

Innocent child and snow-white flower,
Well are ye paired in your opening hour!

JANUARY THIRTY-FIRST

Ye are better than all the ballads

That ever were sung or said,

For ye are living poems

And all the rest are dead.

Longfellow

FEBRUARY

FEBRUARY FIRST

I wonder so that mothers ever fret
At little children clinging to their gown;
Or that the footprints, when the days are wet
Are ever black enough to make them frown,
If I could find a little muddy boot,
Or cap or jacket on my chamber floor,
If I could kiss a rosy, restless foot
And hear it patter in my house once more;
If I could mend a broken cart to-day,
To-morrow make a kite to reach the sky—
There is no woman in God's world could say
She was more blissfully content than I.
Mary Louise Riley Smith

FEBRUARY SECOND

The very souls of children readily receive the
impressions of those things that are dropped into
them while they are yet but soft.
Plutarch

FEBRUARY THIRD

As babes will sigh for deep content
When their sweet hearts for peace make room,
As given, not lent.
Jean Ingelow

FEBRUARY FOURTH

Childhood soberly she wears,
Taking hold of woman's cares
Through love's outreach, unawares.
Lucy Larcom

FEBRUARY FIFTH

I searched for love through many a weary mile,
Till, sick and weary, to my homestead turning
Thou earnest to greet me with a mother's smile
And there upon thy dearest features burning
I saw that love I long had sought in vain.
Heine

FEBRUARY SIXTH

And still the children listed, their blue eyes
Fixed on their mother's face in wide surprise.
Matthew Arnold

FEBRUARY SEVENTH

So we will not sell the Baby!
Your gold and gems and stuff,
Were they ever so rare and precious
Would never be half enough!
For what would we care, My Dearie,
What glory the world put on,
If our beautiful darling was going,
If our beautiful darling was gone.

Selected

FEBRUARY EIGHTH

The happy children! Full of frank surprise,
And sudden whims and innocent ecstacies:
What Godhead sparkles from their liquid eyes.
Edmund Gosse

FEBRUARY NINTH

In him woke
With his first babe's first cry, the noble wish
To save all earnings to the uttermost,
And give his child a better bringing up
Than his had been, or hers.
Tennyson

FEBRUARY TENTH

Children have more need of models than of critics.
Joubert

FEBRUARY ELEVENTH

I wait for my story—the birds cannot sing it,
Not one as he sits on his tree;
The bells can not ring it, but long years oh, bring it
Such as I wish it to be.
Jean Ingelow

FEBRUARY TWELFTH

Thou who didst not erst deny
The mother-joy to Mary mild,
Blessed in the blessed child.
Which hearkened in meek babyhood
Her cradle hymn, albeit used
To all that music interfused
In breasts of angels high and good.
Mrs. Browning

FEBRUARY THIRTEENTH

So sits the while at home the mother well content.
Robert Louis Stevenson

FEBRUARY FOURTEENTH

What use to me the gold and silver hoard?
What use to me the gems most rich and rare?
Brighter by far—aye, bright beyond compare,
The joys my children to my heart afford.
From the Japanese

FEBRUARY FIFTEENTH

Never to living ears came sweeter sounds
Than when I heard thee, by our own fireside
First uttering, without words, a natural tune
While thou, a feeding babe, didst in thy joy
Sing at thy mother's breast.
Wordsworth

FEBRUARY SIXTEENTH

A woman lives

Not bettered, quickened toward the truth and good

Through being a mother?

Mrs. Browning

FEBRUARY SEVENTEENTH

One's early life is certainly a great deal more

amusing to look back to than it used to be while it was

going on.

Anne Thackeray Ritchie

FEBRUARY EIGHTEENTH

When thou hast taken thy repast,

Repose my babe on me;

So may thy mother and thy nurse

Thy cradle also be.

Sing lullaby, my little boy,

Sing lullaby, mine only joy.

Anonymous

FEBRUARY NINETEENTH

Ere thy lips learn, too soon,

Their soft, first human tune,

Sweet, but less sweet than now,

And thy raised eyes to read

Glad and good things indeed,

But none so sweet as thou.

Swinburne

FEBRUARY TWENTIETH

Beat upon mine, little heart! beat! beat!

Beat upon mine! You are mine, my sweet!

All mine, from your pretty blue eyes to your feet.

Tennyson

FEBRUARY TWENTY-FIRST

What is the little one thinking about?

Very wonderful things no doubt!

Unwritten history!

Unfathomed mystery!

J. G. Holland

FEBRUARY TWENTY-SECOND

The real education of children is to keep them at
work and make them unselfish.

Ambrosias

FEBRUARY TWENTY-THIRD

Then be contented.

Thou hast got

The most of Heaven in thy young lot;

There's sky blue in thy cup.

Hood

FEBRUARY TWENTY-FOURTH

Her infancy, a wonder-working charm,

Laid hold upon his love.

Jean Ingelow

FEBRUARY TWENTY-FIFTH

So for the mother's sake the child was dear,
And dearer was the mother for the child.

S. T. Coleridge

FEBRUARY TWENTY-SIXTH

A kiss when the day is over,
A kiss when the day begins,
My mamma's as full of kisses
As a nurse is full of pins.

Selected

FEBRUARY TWENTY-SEVENTH

The child-heart is so strange a little thing,
So mild, so timorously shy and small,
When grown-up hearts throb, it goes scampering
Behind the wall, nor dares peer out at all!
It is the veriest mouse
That hides in any house!
So wild a thing is any child-heart!

James Whitcomb Riley

From "A Child World." Copyright, 1897. Used by special permission of the publishers, The Bobbs-Merrill Company.

FEBRUARY TWENTY-EIGHTH

Out of the dark, sweet sleep

Where no dreams laugh or weep,

Borne through the bright gates of birth

Into the dim sweet light

Where day still dreams of night,

While heaven takes form on earth.

Swinburne

FEBRUARY TWENTY-NINTH

For what are all our contrivings

And the wisdom of all our books

When compared with your caresses

And the gladness of your looks.

Longfellow

MARCH

MARCH FIRST

I am one who holds a treasure
And a gem of wondrous cost;
But I mar my heart's deep pleasure
With the fear it may be lost.

. . . .

Then spoke the Angel of mothers
To me, in gentle tone,
"Be kind to the children of others
And thus deserve thine own."
Julia Ward Howe

MARCH SECOND

Here at the portals thou dost stand
And, with thy little hand,
Thou openest the mysterious gate
Into the future's undiscovered land.
Longfellow

MARCH THIRD

Like children with violets playing
In the shade of the whispering trees.
Charles Kingsley

MARCH FOURTH

Infancy is the perpetual Messiah, which comes

into the arms of fallen men and pleads with them to

return to Paradise

Emerson

MARCH FIFTH

Come to me O ye children!

For I hear you at your play

And the questions that perplexed me

Have vanished quite away.

Longfellow

MARCH SIXTH

A solemn thing it is to me

To look upon a babe that sleeps,

Wearing in its spirit-deeps

The undeveloped mystery

Of our Adam's taint and woe,

Which, when they developed be,

Will not let it slumber so.

Mrs. Browning

MARCH SEVENTH

Some one had left the gate ajar,

Heaven's gate, you know, my dear,

And a baby angel winging by

Peeped out on a scene most drear.

"Oh me!" he murmured in dulcet tones,

"The old Earth needs more light;

I guess I 'll fly a little way

And carry a sunbeam bright."

Selected

MARCH EIGHTH

Dear Babe, that sleepest cradled by my side,

Whose gentle breathings, heard in this deep calm,

Fill up the interspersed vacancies

And momentary pauses of the thought!

My babe so beautiful! It thrills my heart

With tender gladness thus to look at thee.

S. T. Coleridge

MARCH NINTH

When I hustle home at evening,

And the light shines from the door,

An' I see my little baby

Rollin' happy on the floor,

An' see Sister helpin' Mother,

I'm as tickled as can be

An' there aint no King a-livin'

That has got the best o' me.

Judd Mortimer Lewis

MARCH TENTH

O blossom boy! So calm in thy repose!

So sweet a compromise of life and death,

'Tis pity those fair buds shall e'er unclose

For memory to stain their inward leaf,

Tinging thy dreams with unacquainted grief.

Hood

MARCH ELEVENTH

O let thy children lean aslant

Against the tender mother's knee,

And gaze into her face, and want

To know what magic there can be

In words that urge some eyes to dance

While others, as in holy trance,

Look up to Heaven, be such my praise.

Walter Savage Landor

MARCH TWELFTH

Oh, 'tis a touching thing, to make one weep!

A tender infant with its curtained eye

Breathing as it would neither live nor die

With that unchanging countenance of sleep!

Hood

MARCH THIRTEENTH

Two faces o'er a cradle bent;

Two hands above the head were locked,

These pressed each other while they rocked,

Those watched a life that love had sent.

O solemn hour!

O hidden power!

George Eliot

MARCH FOURTEENTH

To see a child so very fair
It was a pure delight.
Wordsworth

MARCH FIFTEENTH

The tree germ bears within itself the nature of
the whole tree; the human being bears within itself
the nature of all humanity, and is not, therefore,
humanity born anew in each child?
Froebel

MARCH SIXTEENTH

Thoughts of all fair and useful things,
The hopes of early years;
And childhood's purity and grace,
And joys that like a rainbow chase
The passing shower of tears.
Bryant

Reprinted from Bryant's Complete Poetical Works by special permission, of D. Appleton & Co.

MARCH SEVENTEENTH

Sweet is the holiness of youth.
Wordsworth

MARCH EIGHTEENTH

All its dainty body, honey sweet,
Clenched hands and curled up feet
That on the roses of the dawn have trod
As they came down from God.
Swinburne

MARCH NINETEENTH

Within my tender mother's arms I sported,
I played at horse upon my grandsire's knee;
Sorrow and care and anger, ill-reported,
As little known as gold or Greek to me.
Baggesen

MARCH TWENTIETH

How do you like to go up in a swing
Up in the air so blue?
Oh, I do think it the pleasantest thing
Ever a child can do!
Robert Louis Stevenson

MARCH TWENTY-FIRST

Sleep, sweet babe! my cares beguiling!
Mother sits beside thee smiling!
Sleep my darling, tenderly!
If thou sleep not, mother mourneth,
Singing as her wheel she turneth;
Come soft slumber, balmily.
S. T. Coleridge

MARCH TWENTY-SECOND

O sweet sleep-angel, throned now
On the round glory of his brow!
Wave thy wing and waft my vow
Breathed over Baby Charley.

I vow that my heart, when death is nigh,
Shall never shiver with a sigh
For act of hand or tongue or eye
That wronged my Baby Charley.
Sidney Lanier

MARCH TWENTY-THIRD

She seemed a thing
Of Heaven's prime uncorrupted work, a child
Of early nature undefiled,
A daughter of the years of innocence,
And, therefore, all things loved her.
Southey

MARCH TWENTY-FOURTH

Bairns and their bairns make sure a firmer tie
Than aught in love the like of us can spy.
Allan Ramsay

MARCH TWENTY-FIFTH

Slumber little friend so wee,
Joy thy joy is bringing.

Bellman

MARCH TWENTY-SIXTH

Thou straggler into loving arms,
Young climber up of knees,
When I forget thy thousand ways
Then life and all shall cease.
Charles Lamb

MARCH TWENTY-SEVENTH

Where children are not, heaven is not, and heaven,
If they come not again, shall be never!
But the face and the voice of a child are assurances
of heaven and its promises forever.
Swinburne

MARCH TWENTY-EIGHTH

O blessed vision! Happy child!
Thou art so exquisitely wild,
I think of thee with many fears
For what may be thy lot in future years.
Wordsworth

MARCH TWENTY-NINTH

And with heaven in their hearts and their faces,
Up rose the children all.
Longfellow

MARCH THIRTIETH

No baby in the house, I know,
'T is far too nice and clean;
No toys, by careless fingers strown,
Upon the floors are seen.
Clara G. Dolliver

MARCH THIRTY-FIRST

The simple lessons which the nursery taught
Fell soft and stainless on the buds of thought,
And the full blossom owes its fairest hue
To those sweet tear drops of affection's dew.
Holmes

APRIL

APRIL FIRST

But Jesus said, Suffer the little children to
come unto me; for of such is the kingdom of
Heaven.
Matt. xix. 14

APRIL SECOND

Sweet and low, sweet and low,
Wind of the western sea,
Low, low, breathe and blow,
Wind of the western sea!
Over the rolling waters go,
Come from the dying moon and blow,
Blow him again to me;
While my little one, while my pretty one sleeps
Tennyson

APRIL THIRD

My mother she's so good to me,
If I was good as I could be,
I couldn't be as good—no, sir!—
Can't any boy be as good as her!

She loves me when I'm glad er sad;
She loves me when I'm good er bad,
An', what's a funniest thing, she says
She loves me when she punishes.

James Whitcomb Riley

APRIL FOURTH

The first train leaves at six P.M.

For the land where the poppy blows,

The mother dear is the engineer,

And the passenger laughs and crows;

The palace car is the mother's arms,

The whistle a low sweet strain,

And the passenger winks and nods and blinks

And goes to sleep on the train.

Edgar Wade Abbott

APRIL FIFTH

In the house of too-much-trouble

Lived a lonely little boy;

He was eager for a playmate,

He was hungry for a toy.

But 'twas always too much bother,

Too much dirt and too much noise:

For the house of too-much-trouble

Wasn't meant for little boys.

Albert Bigelow Paine

APRIL SIXTH

I long for every childish, loving word;

And for thy little footsteps, fairy light,

That hither, thither moved and ever stirred

My heart with them to gladness infinite.

Carmen Sylva

APRIL SEVENTH

A laugh of innocence and joy

Resounds like music of the fairest grace,

And gladly turning from the world's annoy,

I gaze upon a little radiant face

And bless internally the merry boy

Who makes a "son-shine in a shady place."

Hood

APRIL EIGHTH

I had a little daughter

And she was given to me

To lead me gently backward

To the Heavenly Father's knee.

Lowell

APRIL NINTH

Did any one ever tell you

To "stop makin' such a noise,"

When you wuz a-playin' Injun,

An' war-whoopin' with the boys?

Did any one never tell you

Your manners wuz loud and bold?

Then I guess you are one of the grown-ups

And not a boy nine years old.

Exchange

APRIL TENTH

Let us call to mind the years before our little
daughter was born. We are now in the same condition
as then, except that the time she was with us
is to be counted as an added blessing. Let us not
ungratefully accuse fortune for what was given us
because we could not also have all that was desired.
We should not be like misers who never enjoy what
they have but only bewail what they lose.

Plutarch

APRIL ELEVENTH

And I, for one, would much rather;
If I could merit so sweet a thing,
Be the poet of little children
Than the laureate of a King.

Lucy Larcom

APRIL TWELFTH

Ah! Child, what are we, that our ears
Should hear you singing on your way,
Should have this happiness?

Swinburne

APRIL THIRTEENTH

Speak gently to the young,
For they will have enough to bear;
Pass through life as best they may,
'T is full of anxious care.
David Bates

APRIL FOURTEENTH

My Mother's voice! how often creeps
Its cadence on my lonely hours!
Like healing sent on wings of sleep,
Or dew to the unconscious flowers.
I can forget her melting prayer
While leaping pulses madly fly,
But in the still unbroken air
Her gentle tone comes stealing by,
And years and sin and manhood flee
And leave me at my mother's knee.
N. P. Willis

APRIL FIFTEENTH

And then her heart would warm with hope, perhaps,
of what might be to come, of the overwhelming
possibilities—how many of them, to her, lay in
the warm clasp of the child's hand that came pushing
into hers!
Anne Thackeray Ritchie

APRIL SIXTEENTH

The barb in the arrow of childhood's suffering is this: its intense loneliness, its intense ignorance.
Olive Schreiner

APRIL SEVENTEENTH

Like happy children in their play,
Whose hearts run over into song.
Lowell

APRIL EIGHTEENTH

Ah! what would the world be to us
If the children were no more?
We should dread the desert behind us
Worse than the dark before.
Longfellow

APRIL NINETEENTH

Who can tell what a baby thinks?
Who can follow the gossamer links
By which the manikin feels his way
Out from the shore of the great unknown,
Blind and wailing and alone,
Into the light of day?
J. G. Holland

APRIL TWENTIETH

Dear little face, that lies in calm content
Within the gracious hollow that God made

In every human shoulder, where he meant
Some tired head for comfort should be laid.
Celia Thaxter

APRIL TWENTY-FIRST

This three-fold heaven, which you also bear within
you, shines out on you through your child's eyes.
Froebel

APRIL TWENTY-SECOND

Dance little child, oh dance!
While sweet the wild birds sing,
And flowers bloom fair, and every glance
Of sunshine tells of Spring.
Oh! bloom and sing and smile
Child, bird and flower and make
The sad old world forget awhile,
Its sorrow for your sake.
Celia Thaxter

APRIL TWENTY-THIRD

If the golden-crested wren
Were a nightingale, why, then
Something seen and heard of men
Might be half as sweet as when
Laughs a child of seven.
Swinburne

APRIL TWENTY-FOURTH

O little ones whom I have found
Among earth's green paths playing,
Though listening far behind, around,
There comes to me no sweeter sound
Than words I hear you saying.
Lucy Larcom

APRIL TWENTY-FIFTH

A child sees what we are, behind what we wish
to be.
Amiel

APRIL TWENTY-SIXTH

Dear Child! how radiant on thy Mother's knee,
With merry-making eyes and jocund smiles,
Thou gazest at the painted tiles.
Longfellow

APRIL TWENTY-SEVENTH

Our birth is but a sleep and a forgetting:
The soul that rises with us, our life's star,
Hath had elsewhere its setting,
And cometh from afar;
Not in entire forgetfulness
And not in utter nakedness,
But trailing clouds of glory do we come
From God, who is our home.
Wordsworth

APRIL TWENTY-EIGHTH

Happy hearts and happy faces,
Happy play in grassy places,
That was how, in ancient ages,
Children grew to kings and sages.
Robert Louis Stevenson

APRIL TWENTY-NINTH

That wide-gazing calm which makes us older human
beings, with our inward turmoil, feel a certain
awe in the presence of a little child, such as we feel
before some quiet majesty or beauty in the earth or sky.
George Eliot

APRIL THIRTIETH

Her, by her smile, how soon the stranger knows,
How soon by his the glad discovery shows,
As to her lips she lifts the lovely boy,
What answering looks of sympathy and joy!
He walks, he speaks. In many a broken word
His wants, his wishes and his griefs are heard.
And ever, ever to her lap he flies,
When rosy sleep comes on with sweet surprise.
Samuel Rogers

MAY

MAY FIRST

The child whose face illumes our way,
Whose voice lifts up the heart that hears,
Whose hand is as the hand of May.
Swinburne

MAY SECOND

Baby's skies are mother's eyes,
Mother's eyes and smiles together
Make the Baby's pleasant weather.
Selected

MAY THIRD

Oh, when I was a tiny boy
My days and nights were full of joy
Hood

MAY FOURTH

Sweet babe, in thy face
Soft desires I can trace,
Secret joys and secret smiles,
Little pretty infant wiles.
William Blake

MAY FIFTH

For Childhood, is a tender thing, easily wrought

into any shape.

Plutarch

MAY SIXTH

The gilded evenings calm and late
When weary children homeward run.

William Allingham

MAY SEVENTH

Make your children happy in their youth; let
distinction come to them, if it will, after well-spent
years but let them now break and eat the bread of
Heaven with gladness and singleness of heart and
send portions to them for whom nothing is prepared;
and so Heaven send you its grace before meat
and after it.

Ruskin

MAY EIGHTH

The babe by its mother
Lies bathed in joy,
Glide its hours uncounted,
The sun is its toy;
Shines the peace of all its being,
Without cloud, in its eyes,
And the sun of the world
In soft miniature lies.

Emerson

MAY NINTH

In those days life was a simple matter to the
children; their days and their legs lengthened together.
Anne Thackeray Ritchie

MAY TENTH

Timely blossom, infant fair,

Fondling of a happy pair,

Every morn and every night

Their solicitous delight,

Sleeping, waking, still at ease,

Pleasing without skill to please.

Ambrose Phillips

MAY ELEVENTH

Then the face of a mother looks back, through the mist

Of the tears that are welling; and, lucent with light,

I see the dear smile of the lips I have kissed

As she knelt by my cradle at morning and night;

And my arms are outheld with a yearning too wild

For any but God in His love to inspire,

As she pleads at the foot of His throne for her child—

As I sit in the silence and gaze in the fire.

James Whitcomb Riley

*From "Rhymes of Childhood." Copyright, 1890-1898. Used by special permission of the
publishers, The Bobbs-Merritt Company.*

MAY TWELFTH

A child's kiss set on thy sighing lips shall make

thee glad.

Mrs. Browning

MAY THIRTEENTH

I can not say, and I will not say

That he is dead.—He is just away!

With a cheery smile and a wave of the hand,

He has wandered into an unknown land,

And left us dreaming how very fair

It must be since he lingers there.

James Whitcomb Riley

From "Afterwhiles." Copyright, 1903. Used by permission of the publishers, The Bobbs-Merrill Company.

MAY FOURTEENTH

"Rock-a-bye, baby, up in the tree top!"

Mother his blanket is spinning;

And a light little rustle that never will stop

Breezes and boughs are beginning,

Rock-a-bye, baby, swinging so high!

Rock-a-bye.

Lucy Larcom

MAY FIFTEENTH

God's hand had taken away the seal

That held the portals of her speech;

And oft she said a few strange words

Whose meaning lay beyond our reach

Thomas Bailey Aldrich

MAY SIXTEENTH

Happy the child who is suffered to be and content
to be what God meant it to be; a child while
childhood lasts.
Robertson

MAY SEVENTEENTH

When first thy infant littleness
I folded in my fond caress,
The greatest proof of happiness
Was this I wept.
Hood

MAY EIGHTEENTH

His mother's conscious heart o'erflows with joy.
Homer's Iliad

MAY NINETEENTH

For the pure clean wit of a sweet young babe is
like the newest wax, most able to receive the best
and fairest printing.
Roger Ascham

MAY TWENTIETH

At eve the babes with angels converse hold.
Victor Hugo

MAY TWENTY-FIRST

Ilka body smiled that met her,
Nane were glad that said farewell;
Never was a blither, better,
Bonnier bairn frae croon to heel!
MacLeod

MAY TWENTY-SECOND

His father's counterfeit,
And his face the index be
Of his mother's chastity.
Catullus

MAY TWENTY-THIRD

And, rosy from the noonday sleep,
Would bear thee to admiring kin,
And all thy pretty looks would keep
My heart within.
Jean Ingelow

MAY TWENTY-FOURTH

I long to feel thy little arms embrace,
Thy silver-sounding voice to hear,
I long for thy warm kisses on my face,
And for thy birdlike carol, blythe and clear.
Carmen Sylva

MAY TWENTY-FIFTH

All holy influences dwell within
The breast of childhood; instincts fresh from God
Inspire it, ere the heart beneath the rod
Of grief hath bled, or caught the plague of sin.
Sir Aubrey de Vere

MAY TWENTY-SIXTH

The mother represents goodness, providence, law,
that is to say, the divinity, under that form of it
which is accessible to childhood.
Amiel

MAY TWENTY-SEVENTH

Earth's creeds may be seventy times seven
And blood have defiled each creed;
If, of such is the Kingdom of Heaven,
It must be Heaven indeed.
Swinburne

MAY TWENTY-EIGHTH

No song quite worth a young child's ears
Broke ever even from birds in May.
Swinburne

MAY TWENTY-NINTH

And remain through all bewildering,
Innocent and honest children.
Robert Louis Stevenson

MAY THIRTIETH

Before life's sweetest mystery still
The heart in reverence kneels;
The wonder of the primal birth
The latest mother feels.
Whittier

MAY THIRTY-FIRST

O, The days gone by! O, the days gone by!
The music of the laughing lip, the luster of the eye;
The childish faith in fairies, and Aladdin's magic ring—
The simple, soul-reposing, glad belief in every thing.—
When life was like a story, holding neither sob nor sigh,
In the golden, olden glory of the days gone by.
James Whitcomb Riley

*"Rhymes of Childhood." Copyright, 1890-1898. Used by permission of the publishers,
The Bobbs-Merrill Company.*

JUNE

JUNE FIRST

Would ye learn the way to Laughtertown,

Oh, ye who have lost the way?

Would ye have young hearts, though your hair be gray?

Go learn from a little child each day;

Go serve his wants and play his play,

And catch the lilt of his laughter gay,

And follow his dancing feet as they stray,

For he knows the road to Laughtertown

Oh, ye who have lost the way!

Katherine D. Blake

JUNE SECOND

What school of learning or of moral endeavor

depends on its teacher more than the home upon the

mother.

Donald G. Mitchell

JUNE THIRD

What price could pay with earth's whole weight of gold,

One least flushed roseleaf's fold

Of all this dimpling store of smiles that shine

From each warm curve and line?

Swinburne

JUNE FOURTH

Sometimes when I bin bad

An' Pa "correcks" me, nen

An' Uncle Sidney he comes here

I'm allus good again;

Cause Uncle Sidney says,

An' takes me up an' smiles,

The goodest mens they is ain't good

As baddest little childs.

James Whitcomb Riley

JUNE FIFTH

Since then God has willed that children should be

to us in the place of preceptors, we judge that we

owe to them the most diligent attention.

Comenius

JUNE SIXTH

He was so sweet, that oft his mother said,

O, child, how was it that I dwelt content

Before thou camest?

Jean Ingelow

JUNE SEVENTH

Thrice happy state again to be

The trusting infant on the knee!

Who lets his rosy fingers play

About his Mother's neck, and knows

Nothing beyond his Mother's eyes;
They comfort him by night and day,
They light his little life alway.
Tennyson

JUNE EIGHTH

I see in every child the possibility of a perfect man.
Froebel

JUNE NINTH

Where indeed can the modest and earnest virtue
of a woman tell a stronger story of its worth than
upon the dawning habit of a child?
Donald G. Mitchell

JUNE TENTH

The expectant wee-things, toddlin' stacher through
To meet their Dad, wi' flichterin' noise an' glee,
His wee-bit Ingle blinkin' bonnily,
His clean hearth-stone, his thrifty wifie's smile,
The lispin' infant prattling on his knee,
Does a' his weary carking cares beguile,
An' makes him quite forget his labor and his toil.
Robert Burns

JUNE ELEVENTH

To feel sudden, at a wink,
Some dear child we used to scold,

Praise, love both ways, kiss and tease,
Teach and tumble as our own,
All its curls about our knees,
Rise up suddenly full-grown.
Mrs. Browning

JUNE TWELFTH

I thought a child was given to sanctify a woman.
Mrs. Browning

JUNE THIRTEENTH

Under the roof-tree of his home the boy feels safe;
and where, in the whole realm of life, with its bitter
toils and bitter temptations, will he feel safe again?
Donald G. Mitchell

JUNE FOURTEENTH

The heart which plays in life its part,
With love elate, with loss forlorn,
Is still, through all, the child's pure heart
My Mother gave when I was born.
Sully-Prudhomme

JUNE FIFTEENTH

The hyacinthine boy, for whom
Morn well might break and April bloom.
Emerson

JUNE SIXTEENTH

And the mother spoils all her scolding with a
perfect shower of kisses.
Donald G. Mitchell

JUNE SEVENTEENTH

But not a child to kiss his lips,
Well-a-day!
And that's a difference sad to see
Betwixt my lord the king and me.
Charles Mackay

JUNE EIGHTEENTH

There falls not from the height of day,
When sunlight speaks and silence hears,
So sweet a psalm as children play
And sing each hour of all their years,
Each moment of their lovely way,
And know not how it thrills our ears.
Swinburne

JUNE NINETEENTH

But all of the things that belong to the day
Cuddle to sleep to be out of her way;
And flowers and children close their eyes
Till up in the morning the sun shall arise.
Robert Louis Stevenson

JUNE TWENTIETH

O prayer of childhood! Simple, innocent;
O infant slumbers! Peaceful, pure and light;
O happy worship! Ever gay with smiles,
Meet prelude to the harmonies of night;
As birds beneath the wing enfold their head,
Nestled in prayer, the infant seeks its bed.
Victor Hugo

JUNE TWENTY-FIRST

In the little childish heart below
All the sweetness seemed to grow and grow,
And shine out in happy overflow
From her blue, bright eyes.
Westwood

JUNE TWENTY-SECOND

And when she saw her tender little babe,
She felt how much the happy days of life
Outweigh the sorrowful.
Jean Ingelow

JUNE TWENTY-THIRD

Between tears and smiles, the year, like the child,
struggles into warmth and life.
Donald G. Mitchell

JUNE TWENTY-FOURTH

The months that touch, with added grace,

This little prattler at my knee,

In whose arch eye and speaking face

New meaning every hour I see.

Bryant

Reprinted from Bryant's Complete Poetical Works by permission of D. Appleton & Co.

JUNE TWENTY-FIFTH

Come to me, O ye children!

And whisper in my ear

What the birds and the winds are singing

In your sunny atmosphere.

Longfellow

JUNE TWENTY-SIXTH

The adorable, sweet, living, marvellous,

Strange light that lightens us

Who gaze, desertless of such grace,

Full in a babe's warm face.

Swinburne

JUNE TWENTY-SEVENTH

Do not think the youth has no force because he

can not speak to you and me.

Emerson

JUNE TWENTY-EIGHTH

Birds in the night, that softly call,

Winds in the night, that strangely sigh,
Come to me, help me, one and all,
And murmur baby's lullaby.
Lionel H. Lewin

JUNE TWENTY-NINTH

'Tis grand to be six years old, dear,
With pence in a money box,
To ride on a wooden horse, dear,
And leave off baby socks.
F. E. Weatherly

JUNE THIRTIETH

Infancy conforms to nobody; all conform to it,
so that one babe commonly makes four or five out
of the adults who prattle and play to it.
Emerson

JULY

JULY FIRST

A little child, a limber elf,
Singing, dancing to itself,
A fairy thing with rosy cheeks,
That always finds and never seeks,
Makes such a vision to my sight
As fills a father's eye with light.
S. T. Coleridge

JULY SECOND

Bright-featured as the July sun
Her little face still played in,
And splendors, with her birth begun,
Had had no time for fading.
Mrs. Browning

JULY THIRD

The evening star doth o'er thee peep,
To watch thy slumber bright;
My little child, now go to sleep
Safe in God's loving sight.
George Cooper

JULY FOURTH

God promises the children heavenly play,
And blooms in meadows queenly.

Ingemann

JULY FIFTH

But still I feel that His embrace
Slides down by thrills through all things made,
Through sight and sound of every place;
As if my tender mother laid,
On my shut lids her kisses pressure:
Half waking me at night; and said:
"Who kissed you through the dark, dear guesser?"
Mrs. Browning

JULY SIXTH

Even happier than the young wife who feels for
the first time consciousness of her motherhood.
Chateaubriand

JULY SEVENTH

And the least of us all that love him
May take, for a moment, part
With Angels around and above him,
And I find place in his heart.
Swinburne

JULY EIGHTH

The streamlet murmurs on its way;
Dew falls at set of sun;
The birds grow still at hush of day,

So sleep, my little one.
George Cooper

JULY NINTH

The child was happy;
Like a spirit of the air she moved,
Wayward, yet, by all who knew her,
For her tender heart beloved.
Wordsworth

JULY TENTH

My mother's voice, so forgotten yet so familiar,
so unutterably dear!
George Du Maurier

JULY ELEVENTH

But were another childhood-world my share,
I would be born a little sister there.
George Eliot

JULY TWELFTH

With what a look of proud command
Thou shakest, in thy little hand,
The coral rattle, with its silver bells,
Making a merry tune.
Longfellow

JULY THIRTEENTH

Let childhood's radiant mist the free child yet
enfold.

Hemans

JULY FOURTEENTH

Be it, therefore, O mother, your sacred duty to
make your darling early feel the working of both
the outer and the inner light.

Froebel

JULY FIFTEENTH

We do not know
How he may soften at the sight of the child:
The silence often of pure innocence
Persuades when speaking fails.

Shakespeare

JULY SIXTEENTH

Yet nothing is so radiant and so fair
As ——
To see the light of babes about the house.

Euripides

JULY SEVENTEENTH

Through the gladness of little children
Are the frostiest lives kept warm.

Lucy Larcom

JULY EIGHTEENTH

As on the father's care-worn cheek
The ringlets of his child;
The golden mingling with the gray,
And stealing half its snows away.
Holmes

JULY NINETEENTH

There's one angel belongs to you on earth and
that's your mother.
Auerbach

JULY TWENTIETH

Love that lives and stands up recreated,
Then when life has ebbed and anguish fled,
Love more strong than death or all things fated,
Child's and mother's, lit by love and led.
Swinburne

JULY TWENTY-FIRST

Let us live with our children; so shall their lives
bring peace and joy to us; so shall we begin to be
and to become wise.
Froebel

JULY TWENTY-SECOND

And thou, my boy, that silent at my knee,

Dost lift to mine thy soft, dark, earnest eyes,

Filled with the love of childhood, which I see,

Pure through its depths, a thing without disguise.

Hemans

JULY TWENTY-THIRD

Turning to mirth all things of earth,

As only boyhood can.

Hood

JULY TWENTY-FOURTH

A tiny thing,

Whom, when it slept, the lovely mother nursed

With reverent love; whom, when it woke she fed

And wondered at, and lost herself in long

Rapture of watching and contentment deep.

Jean Ingelow

JULY TWENTY-FIFTH

But more sweet

Shone lower the loveliest lamp for earthly feet,

The light of little children and their love.

Swinburne

JULY TWENTY-SIXTH

Full often it falls out, by fortune from God,

That a man and a maid may marry in this world,

Find cheer in the child whom they nourish and care for

Tenderly tend it until the time comes,

Beyond the first years, when, the young limbs increasing,

Grown firm with life's fulness, are formed for their work;

Fond father and mother so guide it and feed it,

Give gifts to it, clothe it: God only can know

What lot to its latter days life has to bring.

Anglo-Saxon Poem

JULY TWENTY-SEVENTH

But children holds he dearest of the dear.

Ingemann

JULY TWENTY-EIGHTH

Brightest and hardiest of roses anear and afar,

Glitters the blithe little face of you, round as a star;

Liberty bless you and keep you to be as you are.

Swinburne

JULY TWENTY-NINTH

We could not wish her whiter—her

Who perfumed with pure blossom

The house—a lovely thing to wear

Upon a mother's bosom.

Mrs. Browning

JULY THIRTIETH

The gracious boy, who did adorn

The world whereunto he was born,

And by his countenance repay

The favor of the loving day.

Emerson

JULY THIRTY-FIRST

Yet the hearts must childlike be,

Where such heavenly guests abide;

Unto children in their glee,

All the year is Christmas-tide.

Lewis Carroll

AUGUST

AUGUST FIRST

Weave him a beautiful dream, little breeze!

Little leaves, nestle around him!

He will remember the song of the trees,

When age with silver has crowned him.

Rock-a-bye baby, wake by and by,

Rock-a-bye.

Lucy Larcom

AUGUST SECOND

Thou art thy mother's glass and she in thee

Calls back the lovely April of her prime.

Shakespeare

AUGUST THIRD

But surely, the just sky will never wink

At men who take delight in childish throe,

And stripe the nether urchin like a pink.

Hood

AUGUST FOURTH

Happy he!

With such a mother, faith in womankind

Beats with his blood, and trust in all things high

Comes easy to him.

Tennyson

AUGUST FIFTH

I have not so far left the coasts of life
To travel inland, that I cannot hear
That murmur of the outer Infinite
Which unweaned babies smile at in their sleep,
When wondered at for smiling.
Mrs. Browning

AUGUST SIXTH

In rearing a child think of its old age.
Joubert

AUGUST SEVENTH

Whither went the lovely hoyden?
Disappeared in blessed wife,
Servant to a wooden cradle,
Living in a baby's life.
Emerson

AUGUST EIGHTH

And yet methinks she looks so calm and good,
God must be with her in her solitude.
Hartley Coleridge

AUGUST NINTH

Childish unconsciousness is rest in God.
Froebel

AUGUST TENTH

The seasons of the year did swiftly whirl,
They measured time by one small life alone.
Jean Ingelow

AUGUST ELEVENTH

Oh, my own baby on my knee,
My leaping, dimpled treasure.
Mrs. Browning

AUGUST TWELFTH

Crazy with laughter and babble and earth's new wine,
Now that the flower of a year and a half are thine,
O, little blossom, O mine and of mine!
Glorious poet who never has written a line!
Tennyson

AUGUST THIRTEENTH

On the lap
Of his mother, as he stands
Stretching out his tiny hands,
And his little lips the while,
Half-open, on his father smile.
Catullus

AUGUST FOURTEENTH

But the breezes of childish laughter,

And the light in a baby's eye,
To the homeliest road bring a freshness
As free as the blue of the sky.
Lucy Larcom

AUGUST FIFTEENTH

My little ones kissed me a thousand times o'er.
Campbell

AUGUST SIXTEENTH

For all its warm, sweet body seems one smile
And mere men's love too vile to meet it.
Swinburne

AUGUST SEVENTEENTH

A child of light, a radiant lass,
And gamesome as the morning air.
Jean Ingelow

AUGUST EIGHTEENTH

Shall we never cease to stamp human nature, even
in childhood, like coins.
Froebel

AUGUST NINETEENTH

My business is to suck, and sleep, and fling
The cradle clothes about me all day long,
Or, half asleep, hear my sweet mother sing,

And to be washt in water clean and warm,

And husht and kist and kept secure from harm.

Shelley

AUGUST TWENTIETH

Golden slumbers kiss your eyes,

Smiles awake you when you rise:

Sleep pretty wantons, do not cry,

And I will sing a lullaby.

Rock them, rock them, lullaby.

Thomas Dekker

AUGUST TWENTY-FIRST

As the moon on the lake's face flashes,

So, happy may gleam, at whiles,

A dream through the dear deep lashes

Whereunder a child's eye smiles.

Swinburne

AUGUST TWENTY-SECOND

Childhood was the bough, where slumbered

Birds and blossoms many-numbered.

Longfellow

AUGUST TWENTY-THIRD

To the royal soul of a baby

One fairy realm is the earth.

Lucy Larcom

AUGUST TWENTY-FOURTH

So rounds he to a separate mind
From which clear memory may begin.
Tennyson

AUGUST TWENTY-FIFTH

I dream of those two little ones at play,
Making the threshold vocal with their cries,
Half tears, half laughter, mingled sport and strife,
Like two flowers blown together by the wind.
Victor Hugo

AUGUST TWENTY-SIXTH

That woman's toy,
A baby!
Mrs. Browning

AUGUST TWENTY-SEVENTH

Perpetual care and joy of our life, our despotic
flatterers, greedy for the very least pleasure, frankly
selfish, instinctively sure of their too legitimate
independence—children are our masters, no matter
how firm we may pretend to be with them.
George Sand

AUGUST TWENTY-EIGHTH

And now, the rosy children come to play,

And romp and struggle with the new-mown hay;
Their clear high voices sound from far away.
Edmund Gosse

AUGUST TWENTY-NINTH

For the house that was childless awhile, and the
light of it darkened, and the pulse of it dwindled,
Rings radiant again with a child's bright feet,
with the light of his face is rekindled.
Swinburne

AUGUST THIRTIETH

My teachers are the children themselves, with
all their purity, their innocence, their
unconsciousness and their irresistible charms.
Froebel

AUGUST THIRTY-FIRST

Women-folks said she was like her father—men-folks
said she was like her mother—but the wisest
people always said she was like us both.
From "The Finest Baby in the World"

SEPTEMBER

SEPTEMBER FIRST

Preserve him from the bad teacher, for
the unfortunate and road-lost one will make
him as himself.
Sa'di

SEPTEMBER SECOND

All unkissed by innocent beauty,
All unloved by guileless heart,
All uncheered by sweetest duty,
Childless man how poor thou art!
Tupper

SEPTEMBER THIRD

We cannot measure the need
Of even the tiniest flower,
Nor check the flow of the golden sands
That run through a single hour.
But the morning dew must fall
And the sun and the summer rain
Must do their part, and perform it all
Over and over again.
Josephine Pollard

SEPTEMBER FOURTH

When you stood up in the house

With your little childish feet,

And, in touching life's first shows,

First the touch of love did meet.

Mrs. Browning

SEPTEMBER FIFTH

Even as a child that after pining

For the sweet absent mother, hears

Her voice, and round her neck, entwining

Young arms, vents all its soul in tears.

Schiller

SEPTEMBER SIXTH

Who takes the children on his knee,

And winds their curls about his hand.

Tennyson

SEPTEMBER SEVENTH

He's such a kicking, crowing, wakeful rogue,

He almost wears our lives out with his noise,

Just at day-dawning when we wish to sleep.

Jean Ingelow

SEPTEMBER EIGHTH

Happy little children, skies are bright above you,

Trees bend down to kiss you, breeze and blossom love you.

Lucy Larcom

SEPTEMBER NINTH

A baby's eyes ere speech begins;
Ere lips learn words or sighs,
Bless all things bright enough to win
A baby's eyes.
Swinburne

SEPTEMBER TENTH

Some day you'll know
How closely to one's heart a son can cling.
Racine

SEPTEMBER ELEVENTH

Thy sports, thy wanderings, when a child,
Were ever in the sylvan wild,
And all the beauty of the place
Is in thy heart and on thy face.
Bryant

Reprinted from Bryant's Complete Poetical Works by permission of D. Appleton & Co.

SEPTEMBER TWELFTH

It was a childish ignorance,
But now 't is little joy
To know I'm farther off from heaven
Than when I was a boy.
Hood

SEPTEMBER THIRTEENTH

Sweet babe! True portrait of thy father's face,
Sleep on the bosom that thy lips have pressed!
Sleep little one; and closely, gently place
Thy drowsy eyelids on thy mother's breast.
Longfellow

SEPTEMBER FOURTEENTH

That land of glorious mystery
Whither we all are wending,
A lonely sort of heaven will be,
If there no baby-family
Await my love and tending.
Lucy Larcom

SEPTEMBER FIFTEENTH

What note of song have we
Fit for the birds and thee
Fair nestling couched beneath the mother-dove?
Swinburne

SEPTEMBER SIXTEENTH

Thou closely clingest to thy mother's arms,
Nestling thy little face in that fond breast
Whose anxious heavings lull thee to thy rest!
Man's breathing miniature.
S. T. Coleridge

SEPTEMBER SEVENTEENTH

A lisping voice and glancing eyes are near,

And ever restless feet of one, who now

Gathers the blossoms of her fourth bright year.

Bryant

Reprinted from Bryant's Complete Poetical Works by permission of D. Appleton & Co.

SEPTEMBER EIGHTEENTH

Once was she wealthy, with small cares,

And small hands clinging to her knees.

Lizette Woodworth Reese

SEPTEMBER NINETEENTH

I, a woman, wife and mother,

What have I to do with art?

Are ye not my noblest pictures,

Portraits painted from my heart?

Margaret J. Preston

SEPTEMBER TWENTIETH

It was a little Child who swung

Wide back that city's portals

Where hearts remain forever young;

And all things good and pure among,

Shall childhood be immortal.

Lucy Larcom

SEPTEMBER TWENTY-FIRST

The mother, with sweet pious face,

Turns toward her little children from her seat,

Gives one a kiss, another an embrace,

Takes this upon her knees, that upon her feet:

And, while from actions, looks, complaints, pretences,

She learns their feelings and their various will,

To this a look, to that a word dispenses,

And, whether stern or smiling, loves them still.

Filicaia

SEPTEMBER TWENTY-SECOND

A living book is mine—

In age three years: in it I read no lies,

In it to myriad truths I find the clue—

A tender little child; but I divine

Thoughts high as Dante's in her clear blue eyes.

Maurice Francis Egan

SEPTEMBER TWENTY-THIRD

That pure shrine

Of childhood, though my love be true

Is hidden from my dim confine.

Author unknown

SEPTEMBER TWENTY-FOURTH

Their glance might cast out pain and sin,

Their speech make dumb the wise;

By mute glad Godhead felt within

A baby's eyes.

Swinburne

SEPTEMBER TWENTY-FIFTH

Lulla-lo! to the rise and fall of mother's bosom
't is sleep has bound you,
And oh, my child, what cosier nest for rosier rest
could love have found you?
Sleep, baby dear,
Sleep without fear:
Mother's two arms are clasped around you.
Alfred Percival Gates

SEPTEMBER TWENTY-SIXTH

And if no clustering swarm of bees
On thy sweet mouth distilled their golden dew,
'T was that such vulgar miracles
Heaven had not leisure to renew:
For all the blest fraternity of love
Solemnized there thy birth, and kept thy holiday above.
John Dryden

SEPTEMBER TWENTY-SEVENTH

Sublimity always is simple
Both in sermon and song, a child can seize on the meaning.
Longfellow

SEPTEMBER TWENTY-EIGHTH

Take thy joy and revel in it,

Living through each golden minute,

Trusting God who gave you this

Baby child to love and kiss.

From "The Finest Baby in the World"

SEPTEMBER TWENTY-NINTH

Still smile at even on the bedded child,

And close his eyelids with thy silver wand.

Hood

SEPTEMBER THIRTIETH

Of such is the kingdom of heaven,

No glory that ever was shed

From the crowning star of the seven

That crown the North world's head,

No word that ever was spoken

Of human or godlike tongue

Gave ever such godlike token

Since human harps were strung.

Swinburne

OCTOBER

OCTOBER FIRST

Little lamb, asleep and still,
God protect thee from all ill;
Those who love thee ne'er can be
Free from pain in loving thee.
From "The Finest Baby in the World"

OCTOBER SECOND

Then, when Mamma goes by to bed,
She shall come in with tiptoe tread,
And see me lying warm and fast
And in the land of Nod at last.
Robert Louis Stevenson

OCTOBER THIRD

How, with a mother's ever anxious love,
Still to retain him near her heart she strove.
Firdausi

OCTOBER FOURTH

Windows of mansions in the skies
Must glow with infant faces,
Or somewhere else in Paradise,
The lovely laughter of their eyes
Lights up all heavenly places.
Lucy Larcom

OCTOBER FIFTH

That pitcher of mignonette
Is a garden in heaven set
To the little sick child in the basement.
Henry Cuyler Bunner

OCTOBER SIXTH

When at morn I first awake,
My mother's face I see,
Smiling and all alight with love
And bending over me.
Mary Stanhope

OCTOBER SEVENTH

We need love's tender lessons taught
As only weakness can;
God hath his small interpreters:
The child must teach the man.
Whittier

OCTOBER EIGHTH

Then, while thy babes around thee cling,
Shalt show us how divine a thing
A woman may be made.
Wordsworth

OCTOBER NINTH

Child of the wavy locks, and brow of light—
Then be thy conscience pure as thy face is bright
Mrs. Browning

OCTOBER TENTH

The thankful captive of maternal bonds.
Wordsworth

OCTOBER ELEVENTH

The mother should consider herself as the child's
sun, a changeless and ever radiant world, whither
the small restless creature, quick at tears and
laughter, light, fickle, passionate, full of storms, may
come for fresh stores of light, warmth and electricity,
of calm and courage.
Amiel

OCTOBER TWELFTH

When grace is given us ever to behold
A child some sweet months old,
Love, laying across our lips his finger, saith,
Smiling with bated breath,
"Hush, for the holiest thing that lives is here,
And Heaven's own heart how near!"
Swinburne

OCTOBER THIRTEENTH

Sweet as the early song of birds,

I heard those first delightful words,
"Thou hast a child."
Hood

OCTOBER FOURTEENTH

And a pretty boy was their best hope, next to the
God in heaven.
Wordsworth

OCTOBER FIFTEENTH

The child soul is an ever bubbling fountain in the
world of humanity.
Froebel

OCTOBER SIXTEENTH

Beware that he weepest, for the great throne of
God keeps trembling when the orphan weeps.
Sa'di

OCTOBER SEVENTEENTH

One thing yet there is, that none
Hearing, ere its chime be done,
Knows not well the sweetest one
Heard of man beneath the sun,
Hoped in heaven hereafter;
Soft and strong and loud and light,
Very sound of very light,
Heard from morning's rosiest height

When the soul of all delight

Fills a child's clear laughter.

Swinburne

OCTOBER EIGHTEENTH

Ere thought lift up thy flower-soft lids to see

What life and love on earth

Bring thee for gifts at birth,

But none so good as thine, who hast given us thee.

Swinburne

OCTOBER NINETEENTH

Childhood had its litanies

In every age and clime;

The earliest cradles of the race

Were rocked to Poet's rhyme.

Whittier

OCTOBER TWENTIETH

Sweet little maid, with winsome eyes

That laugh all day through the tangled hair;

Gazing with baby looks so wise

Over the arms of the oaken chair.

Harry Thurston Peck

OCTOBER TWENTY-FIRST

Everything in immortal nature is a miracle to the
little child.

Anatole France

OCTOBER TWENTY-SECOND

Even so this happy creature of herself
Is all-sufficient, solitude to her
Is blithe society, who fills the air
With gladness and involuntary songs.
Wordsworth

OCTOBER TWENTY-THIRD

The plays of childhood are the heart-leaves of
the whole future life.
Froebel

OCTOBER TWENTY-FOURTH

When e'er you are happy and cannot tell why,
The Friend of the children is sure to be by.
Robert Louis Stevenson

OCTOBER TWENTY-FIFTH

So brief and unsure, but sweeter
Than ever a noon-dawn smiled,
Moves, measured of no tune's meter,
The song in the soul of a child.
Swinburne

OCTOBER TWENTY-SIXTH

Childhood and its terrors rather than its raptures,

take wings and radiance in dreams and sport like
fireflies in the little night of the soul. Do not crush
these flickering sparks!
Richter

OCTOBER TWENTY-SEVENTH

A child should always say what's true
And speak when he is spoken to,
And behave mannerly at table:
At least as far as he is able.
Robert Louis Stevenson

OCTOBER TWENTY-EIGHTH

Bishop Thorold says that whenever a parent
begins to feel virtuous in sacrificing his sleep for his
child, he ceases to love his child. All I can say is
that the Bishop must have kept a night-nurse.
From "The Finest Baby in the World"

OCTOBER TWENTY-NINTH

He it was who bathed the little ones, who "buttoned
up the backs" and tied careful "ribbin bows"
here and there for the whole six; he who drilled them
in "mannerly behavior" in court.

Indeed he had always performed most of these
personal services, which were, so he generously
distinguished them, "acts of love and not labor."
Ruth McEnery Stuart

OCTOBER THIRTIETH

O Wonderland of wayward Childhood! what

An easy, breezy realm of summer calm

And dreamy gleam and gloom and bloom and balm

Thou art!—The Lotus-land the poet sung,

It is the Child-World while the heart beats young.

James Whitcomb Riley

From "A Child World." Copyright, 1897. Used by special permission of the publishers, The Bobbs-Merrill Company.

OCTOBER THIRTY-FIRST

People who write about children should always

tell the truth. For to translate even a child's

simplest day into words is to narrate one of the Seven

Wonders of the world.

From "The Finest Baby in the World"

NOVEMBER

NOVEMBER FIRST

Self-government with tenderness, here
you have the condition of all authority over
children.

Amiel

NOVEMBER SECOND

Heigh ho! Daisies and buttercups!
Mother shall weave them a daisy chain;
Sing them a song of the pretty hedge sparrow,
That loved her brown little ones, loved them full fain:
Sing, "Heart, thou art wide though the house be but narrow";
Sing once and sing it again.

Jean Ingelow

NOVEMBER THIRD

Fair little children, morning-bright,
With faces grave, yet soft to sight,
Expressive of restrained delight.

Mrs. Browning

NOVEMBER FOURTH

Our youth! Our childhood! That spring of springs!
'T is surely one of the blessedest things
That nature ever intended.

Hood

NOVEMBER FIFTH

Ah how good a school is the school of home!
Anatole France

NOVEMBER SIXTH

Loving she is and tractable, though wild;
And innocence hath privilege in her
To dignify arch looks and laughing eyes.
Wordsworth

NOVEMBER SEVENTH

Sweet baby, sleep; what ails my dear?
What ails my darling thus to cry?
Be still my child and lend thine ear
To hear me sing thy lullaby.
My pretty lamb, forbear to weep;
Be still my dear: sweet baby, sleep.
George Wither

NOVEMBER EIGHTH

Through the soft, opened lips the air
Scarcely moves the coverlet.
One little wandering arm is thrown
At random on the counterpane;
And often the fingers close in haste,
As if their baby owner chased
The butterflies again.
Matthew Arnold

NOVEMBER NINTH

I saw her in childhood,
A bright gentle thing,
Like the dawn of the morn
Or the dews of the spring:
The daisies and harebells
Her playmates all day;
Herself as light-hearted
And artless as they.
B. F. Lyte

NOVEMBER TENTH

Thy small steps faltering round our hearth,
Thine een out-peering in their mirth,
Blue een that, like thine heart, seemed given
To be, forever, full of heaven.
Mrs. Browning

NOVEMBER ELEVENTH

Delight and liberty, the simple creed
Of childhood, whether busy or at rest,
With new-fledged hope still fluttering in his breast.
Wordsworth

NOVEMBER TWELFTH

I'd rock my own sweet childie to rest in a cradle
of gold on a bough of the willow,
To the cho-heen-ho of the wind of the west and

the lulla-lo of the soft sea billow.

Sleep, baby dear,

Sleep without fear:

Mother is here beside your pillow.

Alfred Percival Gates

NOVEMBER THIRTEENTH

You too, my Mother, read my rhymes,

For love of unforgotten times;

And you may chance to hear once more

The little feet along the floor.

Robert Louis Stevenson

NOVEMBER FOURTEENTH

And still to childhood's sweet appeal

The heart of genius turns,

And more than all the sages teach,

From lisping voices learns.

Whittier

NOVEMBER FIFTEENTH

The wondrous child,

Whose silver warble wild

Out-valued every pulsing sound

Within the air's cerulean round.

Emerson

NOVEMBER SIXTEENTH

He saw his Mother's face, accepting it
In change for heaven itself, with such a smile
As might have well been learnt there.
Mrs. Browning

NOVEMBER SEVENTEENTH

Heaven lies about us in our infancy!
Shades of the prison house begin to close
Upon the growing boy.
Wordsworth

NOVEMBER EIGHTEENTH

When children are happy and lonely and good,
The Friend of the Children comes out of the wood.
Robert Louis Stevenson

NOVEMBER NINETEENTH

And then, he sometimes interwove
Fond thoughts about a father's love,
"For there," said he, "are spun
Around the heart such tender ties,
That our own children to our eyes
Are dearer than the sun."
Wordsworth

NOVEMBER TWENTIETH

May we presume to say that at thy birth,
New joy was sprung in Heaven, as well as here on earth.

Dryden

NOVEMBER TWENTY-FIRST

Dear five-years-old befriends my passion,
And I may write till she can spell.
Matthew Prior

NOVEMBER TWENTY-SECOND

'T is thus, though wooed by flattering friends,
And fed with fame (if fame it be),
This heart, my own dear mother, bends
With love's true instinct, back to thee.
Swinburne

NOVEMBER TWENTY-THIRD

To prayer, my child! And oh, be thy first prayer
For her, who many nights with anxious care,
Rocked thy first cradle: who took thy infant soul
From heaven and gave it to the world: then rife
With love, still drank the gall of life
And left for thy young lips the honeyed bowl.
Victor Hugo

NOVEMBER TWENTY-FOURTH

Above the hills, along the blue,
Round the bright air, with footing true,
To please the child, to paint the rose,
The Gardener of the World, he goes.

Robert Louis Stevenson

NOVEMBER TWENTY-FIFTH

Children, aye, forsooth,
They bring their own love with them when they come.
Jean Ingelow

NOVEMBER TWENTY-SIXTH

We came upon
A wildfowl sitting on her nest, so still
I reached my hand and touched her: she did not stir;
The snow had frozen round her, and she sat,
Stone-dead, upon a heap of ice-cold eggs,
Look, how this love, this mother, runs through all
The world God made—even the beast, the bird!
Tennyson

NOVEMBER TWENTY-SEVENTH

In your hearts are the birds and sunshine,
In your thoughts, the brooklet's flow.
Longfellow

NOVEMBER TWENTY-EIGHTH

No flower bells that expand and shrink
Gleam half so heavenly sweet,
As shine, on life's untrodden brink,
A baby's feet.
Swinburne

NOVEMBER TWENTY-NINTH

St. Augustine said finely: "A marriage without
children is the world without the sun."

Luther

NOVEMBER THIRTIETH

The child, the seed, the grain of corn,

The acorn on the hill,

Each for some separate end is born

In season fit, and still

Each must in strength arise to work the Almighty will.

Robert Louis Stevenson

DECEMBER

DECEMBER FIRST

As children play, without to-morrow,
Without Yesterday.
Agnes Robinson

DECEMBER SECOND

Shall those smiles be called
Feelers of love, put forth as if to explore
This untried world?
Wordsworth

DECEMBER THIRD

When children are playing alone on the green,
In comes the playmate that never was seen.
Robert Louis Stevenson

DECEMBER FOURTH

Respect childhood and do not hastily judge of it,
either for good or evil.
Rosseau

DECEMBER FIFTH

What does little baby say,
In her bed at peep of day?
Baby says, like little birdie,
Let me rise and fly away.

Baby sleep a little longer,

Till the little limbs are stronger,

If she sleeps a little longer

Baby too, shall fly away.

Tennyson

DECEMBER SIXTH

"Mother," asked a child, "since nothing is ever
lost, where do all our thoughts go?"

"To God," answered the mother, "who remembers
them forever."

"Forever!" said the child. He bent his head and,
drawing closer to his mother, murmured, "I am
frightened!"

Which of us has not felt the same?

Selected

DECEMBER SEVENTH

Happy little children, seek your shady places,
Lark songs in their bosoms, sunshine in their faces.

Lucy Larcom

DECEMBER EIGHTH

The mother, with anticipated glee,
Smiles o'er the child, that, standing by her chair,
And flattening its round cheek upon her knee,

Looks up and doth its rosy lips prepare
To mock the coming sounds: at the sweet sight
She hears her own voice with new delight.
S. T. Coleridge

DECEMBER NINTH

A babe, in lineament and limb
Perfect, and prophet of the perfect man.
Tennyson

DECEMBER TENTH

In the children lies the seed-corn of the future.
Froebel

DECEMBER ELEVENTH

When the bedtime shadows fall,
I'm always sure of this,
Just as I'm drifting off to dreams,
I feel my Mother's kiss.
Mary Stanhope

DECEMBER TWELFTH
Grandma's Prayer

I pray that, risen from the dead,
I may in glory stand—
A crown, perhaps, upon my head
But a needle in my hand.
I've never learned to sing or play,

So let no harp be mine;

From birth unto my dying day,

Plain sewing's been my line.

Therefore, accustomed to the end

To plying useful stitches,

I'll be content if asked to mend

The little Angels' breeches.

Eugene Field

DECEMBER THIRTEENTH

The studying child has all the needs of a creating

artist. He must breathe pure air; his body must be

at ease; he must have things to look at and be able

to change his thoughts at will by enjoying form and

color.

George Sand

DECEMBER FOURTEENTH

At one dear knee we proffered vows,

One lesson from one book we learned,

Ere childhood's flaxen ringlets turned

To black and brown on kindred brows.

Tennyson

DECEMBER FIFTEENTH

Art thou not a sunbeam,

Child, whose life is glad,

With an inner radiance

Sunshine never had?
Lucy Larcom

DECEMBER SIXTEENTH

No rosebuds yet, by dawn impearled
Match, even in loveliest lands,
The sweetest flowers in all the world;
A baby's hands.
Swinburne

DECEMBER SEVENTEENTH

Sweet was the whole year with the stir
Of young feet on the stair.
Lizette Woodworth Reese

DECEMBER EIGHTEENTH

The religion of a child depends on what its father
and mother are, and not on what they say.
Amiel

DECEMBER NINETEENTH

So was unfolded here, the
Christian lore of salvation,
Line by line, from the soul of childhood.
Longfellow

DECEMBER TWENTIETH

It is good to be children sometimes, and never

better than at Christmas, when its mighty founder
was himself a child.

Charles Dickens

DECEMBER TWENTY-FIRST

We greet the joy that Christmas brings;
But, where the heart of childhood sings,
There all the months are full of cheer
And Christmas-tide lasts all the year.

Francis McKinnon Morton

DECEMBER TWENTY-SECOND

Not believe in Santa Claus! You might as well
not believe in Fairies! You might get your Papa
to hire men to watch in all the chimneys on
Christmas Eve to catch Santa Claus, but even if they did
not see Santa Claus coming down, what would that
prove? Nobody sees Santa Claus but that is no sign
that there is no Santa Claus. The most real things
in the world are those that neither children nor men
can see. Nobody can conceive nor imagine all the
wonders that are unseen and unseeable in the world.

From New York "Sun" of Sept. 21, 1897

DECEMBER TWENTY-THIRD

You once told me that in the school of God the
wisest man never gets beyond the Infant Class; I
thought it a strange idea at first but now I know it is

true. For, in the matter of the Eternities, a man's
only hope of learning is to remain in the Infant Class.

Children invariably have the ear of God first. They
have been in His company last.
From "The Finest Baby in the World"

DECEMBER TWENTY-FOURTH

To you this night is born a child
Of Mary, chosen mother mild,
This little child of lowly birth

Shall be the joy of all your earth.

Luther

DECEMBER TWENTY-FIFTH

For unto you is born this day, a Saviour, which is

Christ the Lord. And suddenly there was with the

angel a multitude of the heavenly hosts praising

God and saying, "Glory to God in the highest, and

on earth peace, good-will toward men."
Luke ii. 11, 13, 14

DECEMBER TWENTY-SIXTH

A child is the greatest living revealer of the Eternal
in this world. You are nearer God when you have
your child in your arms than at any other time.
From "The Finest Baby in the World"

DECEMBER TWENTY-SEVENTH

I never realized God's birth before,

How he grew likest God in being born,

This time I felt like Mary, had my babe

Lying a little on my breast like hers.
Robert Browning

DECEMBER TWENTY-EIGHTH

What do I dream of, far from the low roof
Where now ye are children? I dream of you,
Of your young heads that are the hope and crown
Of my full summer, ripening to its fall,
Branches whose shadow grows along my wall,
Sweet souls scarce open to the breath of day,
Still dazzled with the brightness of your dawn.

Victor Hugo

DECEMBER TWENTY-NINTH

Verily I say unto you, "Whosoever shall not

receive the Kingdom of Heaven as a little child

shall in no wise enter therein."
Luke xviii. 17

DECEMBER THIRTIETH

Heroic Mother!

What can breath add to that sacred name?
Author unknown

DECEMBER THIRTY-FIRST

The mother has eternal youth.
Edith M. Thomas

Milton Keynes UK
Ingram Content Group UK Ltd.
UKHW040405160324
439440UK00017B/277